OVERCOMING CHALLENGES

Oteng Montshiti

2

Table of contents

Part 1

Types of challenges-5

Part 2

 How to identify demonic challenges-13

Part 3

How to identify challenges- 16

Acknowledgements

Writing a book is not an easy task. Therefore I would like to thank our lord Jesus Christ, my family especially my lovely wife who supported me.

PART 1

What are the challenges?

Challenges are also known as hindrances, barriers, obstacles, opposition, or stumbling blocks.

Types of challenges

1. Divine tests

These are tests that are ordained or allowed by God to come across your path. God doesn't tempt people but he allows some challenges to come across your path to test your faith in

Him. He knows that everybody can say, "Lord I love you with all my heart" but when the period of testing comes the opposite becomes the case. He always allows them to test your commitment unto him. That's why your relationship with him mustn't be based primarily on material things because if those things aren't available you will ridicule or insults his name.

If you read the book of Job in the Bible you will realize that God blessed him mightily and at the right time God allowed the Devil to attack him. But we thank God because he gave him the grace to endure the attacks to the end and emerged victoriously. What a faithful man unto the Lord. He was tempted not because he had sinned but it was the period of testing his faith in God. God wanted to test if he relating with him because of material gain or unconditionally and he passed the test.

Godly tests are part of your daily walk with the Lord. They are there to strengthen your faith in him. Remember, Christianity is an army of God. The moment you are born again, you are enrolled in Jesus Christ army you must go through vigorous and affective training to serve in his army. Military training isn't meant to destroy people but to transform from a civilian into military mindsets.

In the army, you train throughout your lifetime in there. When I was staying in the city, I would see a group of soldier's everyday singing, running along the road in military uniform, carrying guns, and with a backpack on their backs. Similarly, in Christianity, as long as you are alive, God will always allow obstacles to come across your path to maintain your body, soul, and sprit the way he wants them to be. The word of God compares the life of a true Christian to the life of an Eagle. Eagle is the only bird that loves the storms because it knows that it a blessing in disguise. As a child of God, you should embrace them because, no challenges no growth; and no challenges no promotion or favor.

1Cor 16:9 because a door of great opportunity stands wide open for me, but there are many opponents.

2. <u>Demonic challenges</u>

They are challenges that come from the Devil. They are influenced by demons to kill, destroy your life, and to steal your peace. John 10: 10. Don't think that he loves you. He is your number one enemy. The most dreadful events in this world like genocide, racism, tribal hatred, revenge, wars, and the like Satan is behind them. The beheading and persecution of Christians all over the world, Satan is behind them. That's to say, a demonic hand influences these gruesome events behind the scene.

As a child of God, you must know that Satan will always throw darts at you. Darts can come in the form of fear of the unknown, doubting the potential of God, lack of forgiveness, bitterness, and tormenting you with all manner of pain. Demonic challenges can come in the form of divorces, disobedience of your children, people rejecting you for no valid reason, but be of cheer because God is with you if you hold unto his word.

2Corithians 2:11 so that we may not be exploited by Satan (for we are not ignorant of his schemes).

John 10:10 The thief comes only to steal and kill and destroy; I have come so that they may have life, and may have it abundantly.

PART 2

How to identify demonic challenges

The gift of discernment

The best tool at your disposal as a child of God is the gift of discernment. Discernment means to differentiate what is coming from God or Satan, demons, or angels. If you don't have the spirit of discernment, you are going to think that everything that you are going through is ordained by God while it originates from the pit of hell.

You must read the word of God slowly and meditatively, that is when this gift can be of benefit to you as a believer. Remember, if you lack the truth or Godly knowledge you can't separate errors from the truth. The most powerful to in your arsenal as a child of God is the word of God because discernment simply means comparing what you hear and see with the word of God. If what you are seeing or hearing is not aligned with scriptures you will automatically know that it is not from the Lord.

1 Cor 12:10 to another performance of miracles, to another prophecy, and to another discernment of spirits, to another different kinds of tongues, and to another the interpretation of tongues.

Part 3

How to overcome challenges

Be engaged

The most susceptible person to the devil is somebody who has an idle mind. You must find something useful in life to keep your mind engages. Don't isolate yourself. You should serve in the house of God like cleaning, preparing study materials, and so forth. You should go out there and win souls for the Lord. At the community level, you should get involved in village development projects like talent identification programs, visit the widows and widowers, and visit those who are in prison and hospitals. As you are doing that the burden of worry is lifted from your heart. You start to enjoy every minute of your life and the challenges you are facing become lighter when you join hands with others.

Hospitals and clinics are not built for sick people; there are services there like counseling and many more. You can join support groups in your community where you gather around the table and share experiences and how each one of you is handling his or her situation. As you are doing that you are learning new ideas and how other people are handling their problems in a wisely manner.

Romans 12:11 Do not lag in zeal, be enthusiastic in spirit, serve the Lord.

<u>Make us the internet and social media.</u>

The internet is a powerful tool today; it has turned the world into a global village. When you are facing challenges, make use of Facebook and whattsup. You should join groups that discuss issues you are facing. If you have a marital problem join marital counseling groups and you will lean or two things there.

Today, you can just buy books online and download them on your computer. If you are facing financial dryness search for books which are on free promotion and download them. You can also research online on how to overcome challenges like suicidal thoughts and so forth. You can watch videos on YouTube that motivate you.

Focus on the big picture ahead of you

When challenges come across your path, you should handle them with care. That's to say, you must view them as part of life and that God can't allow temptations that you can't bear to come across your path. Remember that other people are facing similar challenges somewhere in the world. That's enough to give you hope in life.

When they are looming before you, what is going to separate you from the pack is how you view and handle them. Your faith must tell you the greater the challenge the greater the reward. The smaller the challenges, the smaller the reward. You should know that they are just preparing you for the glorious life lying ahead of you.

If you develop a habit of seeing the bigger picture in whatever you are facing, worries and frustration will fade away. You will know in your heart that Jesus Christ is walking with you through trials and tribulations. And that he will reward you handsomely.

Fasting and prayer

The issue of fasting and prayer will always come up because Jesus

Christ told his disciples something they weren't aware of. He told them that some situations aren't solved through prayer alone but a combination of prayer and fasting. When you are facing a seemingly impossible situation fasting and prayer are the keys.

If you are in fasting without praying you are in a hunger strike because the two ingredients work hand and hand. That's to say, one is incomplete without another. When you are fasting and praying please, tell God about it in prayer in advance. You should ask him to give the grace to complete it because during fasting and prayer temptations are very high. For example, people can come and offer you nice food so that you can break it without their knowledge. If you make fasting and prayer an integral part of your Christian life you are already an over comer.

Don't worry about tomorrow

The word of God says you shouldn't worry about tomorrow. Do you know why? It is because the next minute or tomorrow is entirely in the hands of God. Therefore you must clap hands for today's provision and leave tomorrow in the hands of God. The moment you think about what you will eat the next day you are opening the door of worry and frustrations.

I am not saying; sit in your comfort zone. What I am saying is that you should play your part in God's equation and leave him to complete the rest. Most of the time people push things into the hands of God but that's not appropriate. If you are looking for employment send emails, write application letters and God will touch the heart of people to hire you.

Matthew 6:25 Therefore I say unto you, Take no thought for your life, what ye shall eat, or what ye shall drink; nor yet for your body, what ye shall put on. Is not the life more than meat, and the body than raiment?

Matthew 6:26 Behold the fowls of the air: for they sow not, neither do they reap, nor gather into barns; yet your heavenly Father feedeth them. Are ye not much better than they?

Matthew 6:27 Which of you by taking thought can add one cubit unto his stature?

Matt 6:28 And why take ye thought for raiment? Consider the lilies of the field, how they grow; they toil not, neither do they spin:

Matthew 6:29 And yet I say unto you, That even Solomon in all his glory was not arrayed like one of these.

Matthew 6:30 Wherefore, if God so clothe the grass of the field, which to day is, and to morrow is cast into the oven, *shall he* not much more *clothe* you, O ye of little faith?

Matthew 6:31 Therefore take no thought, saying, What shall we eat? or, What shall we drink? or, Wherewithal shall we be clothed?

Matthew 6:32 (For after all these things do the Gentiles seek :) for your heavenly Father knoweth that ye have need of all these things.

View them as part of life

Challenges are part of life, and none of us can escape from them. That's to say, they come across everybody's path whether you are black or white. They are not discriminatory. Many folks have come into the kingdom of God with the wrong mentality, thinking that they will be free from challenges. Well, they are wrong. When you are a child of God, you become a threat to the kingdom of darkness and Satan will not sit down somewhere in the shadows with his head buried between his knees. He is going to fight you like never before.

Even people who are not born again Satan fights them because he doesn't want them to be born again or he wants them to die outside the kingdom of God. If you die outside the kingdom of God he knows that you are going to join him in hell. That's the biggest challenge none believers are facing in their lives. He uses things like drug addiction, sexual immorality, and criminal activities to bind them to himself. The best method to solve this challenge is to be born again and start serving the Lord.

They are temporary

One thing is certain in this world, nothing lasts forever. That's to say, challenges are temporary. They come, go and new ones are introduced in your life to elevate you further into the realm of greatness. If you are swimming in a pool of financial dryness be of good cheer because a season of financial abundance is coming your way. If you are going through shame, the season of glory is around the corner. If you are barren, the time of carrying your baby is at the doorstep. If you are in prison, don't worry your season of freedom is just looming in the horizon ahead of you.

The word of God says, sorrow may come in the night but joy comes in the morning.

2Corithians 4:18 because we are not looking at what can be seen but at what cannot be seen. For what can be seen is temporary, but what cannot be seen is eternal.

The end

Lightning Source UK Ltd.
Milton Keynes UK
UKRC011023031120
372688UK00015B/204/J

* 9 7 8 1 7 1 5 6 6 6 0 6 4 *